# AN INSOMNIAC'S SLUMBER PARTY WITH MARILYN MONROE

HEIDI SEABORN

First Edition
1 2 3 4 5 6 7 8 9

Cover photo: Photographed by Milton H. Greene © 2020 Joshua Greene • www.archiveimages.com

Cover design by Sasha Ori
Interior design by Jojo Rita

ISBN 978-1-948587-19-8

PANK Magazine
PANK Books

To purchase multiple copies or book events, readings and author signings contact info@pankmagazine.com.

# AN INSOMNIAC'S SLUMBER PARTY WITH MARILYN MONROE

HEIDI SEABORN

*~ To Scott, for being there through every volta.*

Heidi Seaborn is author of the acclaimed *Give a Girl Chaos (see what she can do)* and Comstock Chapbook 2020 prize winning *Bite Marks*. She's won or been shortlisted for dozens of awards and her work has been widely published. She's the Executive Editor of *The Adroit Journal.* heidiseabornpoet.com

Also by Heidi Seaborn

Books of Poetry
*Give a Girl Chaos {see what she can do}*

Chapbooks
*Bite Marks*
*Finding My Way Home*
*Once a Diva*

*"Who said nights were for sleep?"*
~Marilyn Monroe

# Table of Contents

*Insomnia Diary

# Insomnia Diary

1:28 am

I've taken Ambien every day this week. On Tuesday a quarter tab,
by Thursday, a half. My pillow bucks. Crows peck the skylight
& the moon's a neon fog. My love breathes through his mouth—flaming a fire.
I close my eyes to the smoke but sparks remain.

# Marilyn

She arrives: a gardenia in a cellophane box,
petals of honeyed hair radiating.
Each blade of light travels the bud
of her dimpled chin. How like a child,
holding a buttercup to know the future.
It's all there, in the corsage of her lips.
Teeth like snowdrops emerging after
the last frost. Her cheeks a landscape
of peonies not yet weighted
by the heaviness of their heads.
The Internet loves her. & I love
how lashes brush the sky of her face
like a bough sprung & her eyes—
blooming only now.

I see her everywhere—


On the wall of a cowboy bar in Wyoming,
a photo of Marilyn in a potato sack. Naked

legs like a chorus girl. IDAHO spanning
her breasts, POTATOES cinching her waist,

100 LBS. NET marking her pubis, marking her
as a bag of produce, to be slit open, dumped

into a bin, priced and purchased. To be
someone's mash, soup, fries, rolled in tin

& baked until she steams when sliced
with a knife from end to end, butter seeping.

The photo marked: 1951, courtesy
Fox Studios Dept. of Publicity.

*Reticular activating factor* says my mother.
*She's on your brain.* I let her stay
in my head for a while—

I prop Warhol's *Marilyn Monroe, 1967*
postcard on my desk.
We stare at one another.

Her eyelids smeared with raspberry,
her mouth a smashed plum.

## What I Give of Myself

It used to bother me
when people I didn't know touched
me   they haven't
loved me     no not really
they say *Marilyn*   touch me
as if we are friends  lovers
as if  we hadn't seen each other
in forever    & now the whiff of me
the scent of me    they feel belongs
to them   just don't
let them see me sweat    the flush
rushing up my throat as they push
into my body    a body that is not
my body
these days    I don't recognize myself
a photograph      black & white   a flash
so I do what I always do what I have to
the press   of a wallet   the pressure
I turn & smile   blow a kiss
that is really nothing
a transaction of air

Refusing to Bow

Marilyn's been so accommodating—smiling
in her winning   winsome   way

for decades now
& now
on Instagram & Twitter
O the things said
@marilyn.

Really.
Friends even. Take Capote.
He knew to steer her by the elbow into a bar
to slowly slip her secrets
down his throat
then parade her
like a poodle leashing along Lexington.

Or Miller. O Arthur
you should've buried her off stage.

*Poor thing*
the tourists mutter    posing
by her crypt.

She is a selfie.

Such are the physics of living
larger than life.
Even Pauline Kael wrote *I wish they'd let her die.*

But here she is  still
jiggling & giggling

on YouTube

      refusing to bow
to the bitch
that is gravity
that is the grave.

## Snapping a Selfie

I would like to say something to the woman
I've known since I was that red-haired girl.
I only borrowed this smile for the day. I know
it's a little worn, torn at the seams. You see, I
hardly know what to do with myself, but lipstick helps.
Paint my mouth like a bed of zinnias—orange,
hot pink, fire red & pretend I'm summer.
I'll invite everyone I know over and we'll jump
in the pool, splash around in my blue eyes.
In a blink, we are all smoking cigarettes behind
the vending machine & dropping dimes for soda pops.
I have a sinking feeling that this moment
is already gone where the extinct
animals go to get catalogued, a flash
in the pan like the Aerocar or the hydrogen bomb
or gold nail polish. All that glimmers is what
keeps me up at night. But last night was a blur.
Isn't it always that way when you wake up and look
in the mirror at who you were yesterday?
Some days, it's best to stay in bed way past
when the robins have gone.

2:42 am

I could wander the halls with Marilyn tonight. I want
a cigarette & a push-up bra to make it through.

# Blonde is a Color

Should I describe her in color: honey,
champagne, the fading

lemon wedge of a horizon
before it melts into midnight blue,
or milk gone sour?

Mailer called her "sweet
bursting peach,"
having never met her.

His fantasy:
that he could save her from other
men like him.

Practicing lines off set,
she knew hot pink hunger—
coiling in her stomach,
burning her throat.

That's how Warhol painted her—
violent bursting pomegranate,
staining the ivory shag carpet.

What color will I choose? Tulip red?
Indigo blue like a Japanese robe
or the lupine in my garden.

Or is she black like a spider
suspended,
holding steady against the breeze.

Perhaps she is happiest there,
out of view,
watching.

# Shadows

**1**

Above me helicopters buzzed the constant cerulean sky as OJ and his friend drove back to Brentwood in the white Bronco, shadows flickering. Two weeks before, we had moved into a little house on Shetland Lane gaudy with bougainvillea and hibiscus. Nicole lived at the far end of Shetland before moving to the townhouse where she died beside a white oleander.

**2**

People arrived from New Zealand and Arizona to hold prayer vigils under the fiery bottle brush tree in front of Nicole's old house. At the other end—a cul-de-sac where our children rode tricycles.

**3**

Beyond the cul-de-sac's dead end—a wooded hill and beyond that, Marilyn's home. The one she died in, on Fifth Helena. Sometimes I walked with my children, pushing the baby's stroller, the long way to 12304 Fifth Helena. The olive tree that must have hovered above Marilyn's head now fully grown, reaching over the white brick wall. I'd always say a little prayer there, not knowing why.

**4**

For a long time, blue-uniformed police guarded OJ's house. I'd walk the children to the church preschool, passing the murder scene hidden by the white oleander and cordoned by yellow tape.

**5**

When our neighbor testified at the trial, the tabloid press ridiculed her for saying, "I know when they had the argument because OJ parked his car in front of our house under the jacaranda. It was in bloom. And I remember as he drove off angrily, the blue violet petals scattering."

**6**

I witnessed the jacaranda bloom every April, and briefly again in the fall before climate change. The children and I would drive this one street in

Beverly Hills lined with jacaranda. We'd roll the windows down, catch their flutter in our fingers, singing "What if God was One of Us" loudly, off key.

7

In 1996, when I took a new job making a bit more money, we moved North of Sunset, up the hill onto Tigertail. We had an arbor of electric blue morning glory and hydrangea. It was always summer. I ripped up the carpet, installed cobalt floors. Beyond the arbor, over the back fence, an old woman who taught acting to Marilyn Monroe was slowly dying in her white shuttered house. I didn't think to pray for my neighbor.

8

On a full moon, I'd cast coins into the pool. As the children dove—sleek, golden bodies and the magnolia bloomed at the pool's edge. The night air stirred with lemon and chlorine.

9

Years later, we found ourselves in the garden of a sapphire blue house in Marrakesh and I longed for the oasis of our old home with its cobalt floors, when the children were little and lived like fish.

10

If you fly over L.A. in an airplane it looks like this: fragments of turquoise sea glass like fingerprints on a landscape of sand, carved by streets shiny with cars like beetles or mirrors shisha-stitched into a dress. Its hem, a flounce of white sand and waves before everything falls away into the blue, blue ocean. Distance is an aphrodisiac. I flew away often.

## Marilyn in the Tea Leaves

You were never my thing,                          so past tense—

You were dead even then,                          and unknowable.

A relic really—your pink leather makeup case, hips swinging, inflating the air.

What do you have to say                          for yourself?

# What We Say For Ourselves
*~ "One in 16 American women's first sexual intercourse experience is rape."*
*JAMA Internal Medicine Study, September 2019*


O darling, before I was blonde as sunshine,

I was a strange girl
     in a home of strangers,

schooled by a man
who called himself
        *Daddy.*
I baked him a whole pie.
He sliced it into fractions—
     The fruit softening
        before the knife,

juice of furred berries blackening the tin.

I remember the next morning. When I opened the curtains—

the green garden dulled, as if someone hadn't dusted.

Brambles thickened the chain link fence, berries fallen & rotting.

I've buried the memory like a bone.


\*\*\*


Marilyn,

I remember clumps of dandelions as if colored by a child.

Above, smudged *Sky Blue & Baby Powder* clouds.

13

*Blue Jean* cut offs. His skin was *Lumber*. I could pick him out of a Crayola box.

Even now decades later, when sometimes
I forget what happened yesterday—

## O Breasts

O fat
& dumb
& white—

O precious tickets
to a carnival.
Cotton candy.
Disneyland Matterhorn
roller coaster.

O show stealers—
main stage act,
I'm your back-up singer.

O tricksters—
how dare you
pretend
to guard a heart.

# Hey

apple, ass, anchor,

bitch, blonde, bombshell, beauty, babe, baby, blossom, bug, bird, bubblehead,

child, chick, creampuff, cherry, cookie, cock tease, cunt,

darling, dear, dog, daddy's girl, dirty girl, demon, divorcée, dangerous, drug,

evil, exotic, everything,

fix, fling, flower, femme fatale, floozy, fox, fondle, fuck

girl, goddess, gift, gal,

heart, heartache, headache, hottie, honey, honeybee, heaven, hard-on, hellcat,

ice queen,

jewel, juice, joy, joke, jam,

kittycat, kid, kiss,

lady, lazy, loose, love, lover,

mistress, maid, momma, mother, Madonna, mouth, mink,

narcotic, nurse, nutcase,

oyster, oh baby,

pearl, prick tease, plump, pin-up, prostitute, prize, pushy

queen, quest,

royal pain in the ass, rape bait, raw, romp,

sexy, skirt, shag, screw, smooch, smokin', spank, sport, sugar, sweetheart,

tits, tart, tease, temptation, trifle, tail, thing,

ugly

vagina, valentine, virgin, vow, vixen,

whore, woozy, woman, womb, wet, wild thing,

x as in x-rated, x-ray, my fuckin' ex,

you,

zero

# Becoming Marilyn

*Marilyn*
*Mar a lyn*  her  lips
almost kiss
tongue slides
behind front teeth
       mouth of running water
a baptism
*Marilyn*


In the mirror
Norma Jeane arches Marilyn's brow


From then on, whenever she thrusts a hip
she will hear someone
 call
      *Marilyn*

traffic slowing

& when she turns to wave
gloved hand tipped
at the wrist
      her smile will press
her cheekbones into stones.

## 1:46 am


My Ambien's in a pill box purchased from the gift shop
at Frida Kahlo's blue home. Frida lay in that bed with Diego
pinned butterflies brushing overhead. I breathe quietly as a ghost.
When the outside world murmurs, my heart revs its little engine—
addicted to adrenaline—if I slow my breathing
will it slow, tamping the brakes as it corners?

Work

When opportunity failed to arrive like a taxi,

I left home—
        a head of steam.

Took to haunting the clouded rooms
—English leather, dark oak
cigar smoke.

On stiletto heels, we could see
        the cards men held, the deck
        long ago stacked
        in the dealer's favor.

Skirting around the board room,
        we forgot our places,
                elbowed a seat. The table
        already set against us.

But I bury my lede as women often do,
        fashion a story—
                charm becomes armor—

        We were armed. They were
                disarmed.

        Our lilting voices disturbing

the papers piled on their desks, shuffling
        their order into mine.

# Reading Ulysses
*~From an Eve Arnold photograph*


Scholars call it parallax me reading Joyce
I say pair a legs to that mine & Molly's
our skirts blowing up showing cream
muslin drawers I wore white cotton
panties two pair doubled up for the scene
that incited Joe to *treat me like dirt* yes
that's what I was reading when everyone
assumed I was reading only the dirty
parts so that's what they wrote in the
paper about me reading my first edition
that I bought at the Strand and carried
everywhere so while the photographer
was fiddling with the film I pulled it
out to read and when she asked me if I
liked it I said it's a slog which everyone
knows it is but it's a bigger slog to be
*always in the kitchen to get his lordship
breakfast* and it's a huge slog to break
with the studio move across country
& start your own production company
now that's a slog so when I slog through
*Ulysses* it's because I might just option
it hire a writer any director I want and
play the role of Molly *I don't care what
anybody says itd be much better for the
world to be governed by the women in it
you wouldn't see women going and killing
one another slaughtering when do you ever
see women rolling around drunk like they
do or gambling every penny they have and
losing it on horses yes because a woman
whatever she does she knows where to stop.*

## Selfie with Marilyn Monroe
*~after Diane Seuss*


—cucumber slices & ice & a compress
—~~a diaphragm~~
—Anne Sexton, a cigarette, vodka
—contract & divorce lawyers on speed dial
—ice. did I say ice? lemon peeler
—the roll up stockings I once wore
—a leisurely lap in the swimming pool
—Jimmy Choo shoes
—Ambien & dental floss
—the cliché of a hand mirror
—the garter & the man I wore them for
—do clocks still tick?
—~~gardenia~~ champagne in the fridge, you never know
—this isn't about her
—anti-aging cream & mascara
—I too have lived on that glittering edge

1:26 am


I'm patrolling tonight's borders
for a scrap of sleep to roll & smoke.
I crave Ambien & a limey vodka tonic.
It's the middle of the night & Marilyn's here

without a lick of makeup in my kitchen,
wrapped in a cream silk robe. Like mine.
So many men & marriages between
the two of us it's hard to keep track—

I offer her tea. She opts for that vodka, says
*Skip the Ambien darling, we have things to discuss.*

# After the Honeymoon

Darling, if your second marriage is anything
like mine,

you will be invited to his mother's home
to crush the garlic, swirl the sauce to a simmer, whisk

eggs, cream, babies.
You will hush your cry. Reduce

your glamour to a glimmer.
Slip your high heels under his bed; walk barefoot

into his story. Its glory fading
in the flash of lights, cameras, red carpet
under your manicured toes.

I dare you to hold that pose—
his arm shielding against your fame rising.

Do you remember wanting a man
to love you into oblivion?

When you lift the skirt of your dreams, will he
applaud?

## Second Marriage

I studied his name on the university building
I'd studied in. Studied the dark writing
when his mother issued eggshell
invitations, stiff & engraved.
I obeyed, said yes to the litany
of cocktails & Sunday dinners.

Kept quiet, kept quietly working,
kept quietly building
a name. He wanted me
kept. His work pressing
a thumb on mine. His
thumb pressing on my eggshell
throat. How angry
my flesh.

How my angry flesh worried
the marriage thin.
How I worried the thin
nights, worried myself
so very thin—
a litany of worries
forming
in my throat,
pressing into
prayers

engraved—
on my eggshell
flesh. I kept
quiet.

Until another man.
Until another man issued a darker invitation.
I said yes.

The Affair

A party—
Stepping out into the jasmine night.
She'd read his latest play. He'd seen her movies.

When his letters arrived like weather,
she wore a coat in summertime.

Seasons leafed along like that.
He appeared one evening wearing

the tie his wife had knotted.
They had dinner.

Windows closed around them.
Their candlelit bodies shuttered.

When morning sunk her teeth,
they drank each other again,

the day severed from all
others. They collected

these days into a home with no keys.
She bathed in his voice—

words slipping down the drain
into his palms.

They washed themselves, their history—
bedsheets billowing. They forgot

how a clothesline tells a story to
strangers, the neighbors, his wife

passing by on a Sunday drive.
They gathered up their cottoned days

& walked out into the afternoon sun
together, blinking.

How to Throw a Communist Party
*~from Marilyn's party menu notes*

*Champagne? At least some kind of wine with dinner Buy*—*liquor*—*scotch*—*gin*—*vermouth*—*Hors d'oeuvres*—*caviar*—*Others?* Is that Copeland on the turntable?—*Marilyn are you cooking up a Communist plot?*—Wanna Martini Comrade George?—& what can I get you dear Comrade Marsha? Here, have some nibbles! Maybe an olive or two? Care for a refresh? napkin? *Celery hearts*—*scallions?*—*Radishes.* Are the crudités Unsalted?— Izzy you look so devilish, your hair slicked back like Stalin & knocking back a Manhattan— Never mind!—Have you seen *Forbidden Planet?* Red flick alright & red monsters—*Two roasts*—*red meat!*— I dare say, *prime ribs of beef*—anyone heard about Chaplin?—*turkey*—the *Times* called Bridge a turkey— Silly that!—Hedda darling will you make the dressing—*large mixed green salad with endive hearts*—avocado? The Hollywood Ten gang—*(Also aspic)*—in Mexico? Marilyn this is divine—*vegetables*—*frozen peas or in Pod?*—A drink to Art & Marilyn! Two perfect peas in a pod—*Or Potatoes*—& I hear Orson's having an Affair—Hey dreamboat—more red wine? it's French—*fruit & ice cream for dessert*—*choc & vanilla Norman,* Recite a poem pretty please!—have some *Coffee & cookies & Danish pastry*—Jessie you're awfully quiet. I'll Take a White Russian & *later Birthday cake for Helene*—let's sing Happy Birthday & make a great big wish! You didn't!—Leave the dishes—& roll up the rugs! I've got Robeson's new record. C'mon let's dance!

There Was No Honeymoon


*You ever think of getting married again?* & there it is just like the dog's vomit
that everyone steps around. O, I loved Art alright. Willing him free from
McCarthy's clutches, I said I do, said yes to be a stamp on his passport. So,
if your third marriage is anything like mine you will call him *Daddy*

& discover
he has written
your dialogue
in the margin.
Everything's
been scripted.
But don't I love
being told
what to do?
There is a fork
for every course
& I knew at night
to let him spoon
'the sweet
cantaloupes
of my rump'.
I knew to
disappear into
his white curtain
Connecticut,
appear for
cocktails with his
curious friends.
Isn't she a wonder ?
I knew to quit
work, to make
babies & when
he drew a blank
page from his
typewriter, I

knew to bury
my unborn
& go back
to work.

In the hole,

I dug another hole
& that was my heart
filled with fish heads
broken sparrows   mold
box wine & accusations
I poured everything down
a drain clogged with my long hair
I could hear mice scratching
beneath the sink  how low
I'd go   I watched a man beg
& knew to shovel deeper   down
where the earth kicks up heat
where liars gather to chew the fat
where I could lounge comfortably
in my recliner   stretching
the truth like a politician
or a serial adulterer or a husband
drunk in the middle of the day
for this is what we've come to
two cowards playing Texas
Hold'em    & calling it
love.

In that hole,

I dug another hole
& that was my heart
edged with silver   thin
as a dime fragile as
fish scales   a heart brimming
with so much milk I swam
laps & dove like a dolphin
beneath the surface I discovered
cities made of Legos & doll
house suburbs where we drove
Hot Wheels around in crazy loops
I lived there with my babies
the tub overflowing with
heavenearthwater   I locked
the door to strangers
a man begging at the tide
it was a time of counting moons
the horizon a wound & the cruelty
of squalls   I gathered our
auras green & golden
when the wind changed
we jibbed & called it
love.

4:07 am


Scene: The baby cries, I never sleep. The LA light so bright.
The sky lit in a ducky night light glow. Always awake
in my teeming house, the walls whistling.

Dissolve to: did *she* feel this constant whirr—
no baby to tend to, to pretend to be awake for?
Awake at four in her dead house.


Then a scarlet bird, like an omen. I don't know what kind.

# What the Maid Witnessed

Mrs. Miller alone at the kitchen table, writing, a cup of tea
> *She remembers—her pale chiffon dress*

pink robe
> *that she wore on a windy afternoon when she walked*

feathers fluttering at her wrists like cherry petals
> *where no one had ever been*

fingers curl a pencil
> *her clear-eyed baby who lived to die*

hair the color of her milky tea
> *The woman stares*

confetti of tears
> *& stares in space*

## Lost Angeles

Outside, hibiscus blooms
the color of raspberries.

We made her in this bungalow.
Tiny pink-throated hummingbird.

The doctor wore pink, I think.

"Would you like a cup of tea?"
The playwright writes the line.

It is dialogue; and I say, "Yes dear,
tea with bread and jam please."

Then I remember jam spread
on the bedsheets.

In the cold of morning
I've held a hummingbird

like an egg, wings stilled.

# Loss

The sky is the color of the sea is the color of my house is the color of worry is the color of quiet is the color of mourning is the color of smoke is the color of an envelope is the color of a face after death is the color of the seagull flapping its wings into the color of winter & winter is the absence of color of rubbed out or forgotten or muted or buried or bleached or boiled or erased or stolen away with night or lost through the hole in a pocket or between the seats of the car or in the chaos of a move or in the laundry or in translation when we try to say something kind & what comes out is noise like the color of the sky & the color of the sea & the color of weather of exposure of erosion coloring me numb coloring me vague coloring me.

After the Miscarriages

My dearest Marilyn, I feel so vacant
I can barely write, like a balloon deflated
or a home emptied of its furniture, just dust

furring the floors, the sunlit windowpanes.
But weren't we the tops once—the Macy's
Day Parade, all brassy bands, floats and flags.

I never loved you more than when I was bent
over my typewriter, punching out words
for you. Never loathed you more—

the muse of you consuming me. You burn
so brightly and then darken. In this house
of hyacinths and cocktails and a shuttered

nursery, the lights flicker at night mimicking
your breath. You sleep the sleep of the dead—
and I wonder how to write you a new ending.

I wonder how to write anything at all as
paper blackens to ash, crumbles to cinders
then levitates in the smoke up the chimney.

                              Love, Art

## Postcard from Reno

Dear Art,

There is no beauty in this land. Dirt & sky.
Nothing in between. Just a thin line—
a demarcation of heaven from earth.

You once called me nightly from here—
forced by divorce into this desert.
Our love, a red-tailed hawk.

& now here I am, playing at love.
Shacked up in an empty landscape—
with a shadow of you.

Shadows lengthen with the day—
& at night the stars bury one another.
When we wrap, it's over, it's over, it's over.

                                        -M

## 3:19 am


17th night awake. Sirens flare all night.
The Frida box beside the bed, pills pre-cut.
Lick my finger, a half Ambien sticks.
On my tongue, tin. I knot a poem
into a scarf, loop it around my throat.

*Divine Marilyn* in Paris
*~July 2019*


Here you are in my jetlag
on Rue des Ecoles.
Your dress fanning open
into a white lily,
arms like stamen,
grinning for all of Paris.

I cross the street.
I'm tired
of chasing you like a rabbit.

But you're everywhere.
*Divine Marilyn* smacked
onto every bus stop, metro, café.
You are what to do in Paris:
*200 clichés de Marilyn Monroe réunis à Paris cet été.*

\*\*\*


I am alone in Galerie Joseph with Marilyn.

Her eyebrows bridge from wall to wall.
Her body of work spreading limber legs
from one room to the next.

*Tête á tête*, I gaze into her gaze.
But she looks beyond me
to another photograph of Marilyn
looking at another photograph of Marilyn.
I'm in a mirrored labyrinth
of Marilyn.

\*\*\*

Next to a Bert Stern portrait,
I take a selfie.
We both wear black dresses,
hair pulled back in a chignon.

The air stirs as if breathing.

I inhale, pull out a pen &
together we
rewrite the exhibition notes.

*[1929—Norma Jeane, age 3, with her mother]*

Momma came & made promises
but stuffed me in a closet.

"Don't make so much noise, Norma"
I was a brown quiet mouse.

Momma fell down the stairs.
Her head broke open.

*[1932—Norma Jeane at age six]*

It was Los Angeles
& our street was a bag
of saltwater taffy bought
on the boardwalk for a nickel.
I didn't have a nickel

but I lived in a mint green
farmhouse across the street
from the pink bubble gum house
that belonged to my grandma.

She & Momma went crazy & left me
with the goats, chickens & a herd
of foster kids. We sold brown eggs,
apples, plums, lemons & watermelon
from our stand.

I climbed the big fig tree,
watched for Momma's return.

*[1934—Norma Jeane at age 8]*

I was never the girl you keep
like a bowl on a shelf.
This house. My bowl—
the littlest, mustard
yellow, chipped on its lip
with a crack down the side
that sweated soup when us kids
elbowed round the Formica table.

*[1935—Los Angeles Orphans' Home Society]*

The sun cut sharp
angles down that scratch
of dirt road, stopped
short of the stone building.
Someone had painted the inside
walls sidewalk grey,
ordered metal tables,
chairs, beds, toilets. Sheets—
once white now laundered winter grey.
Every day I'd run
outside into the lit sky.
Lie on a patch of green
weeds before walking
to the cinderblock school.
Its walls were covered with maps—
countries the color of saltwater
taffy like my first
remembered home.

*[Photo of Charles Stanley Gifford Sr., undated]*

I will haunt this man, my father.
Be his last dream as night unspools
into day. I will be the white shadow
on his gleaming forehead, slick in his hair,
shaving nick on his throat.

I want to hollow his chin with my knuckle,
slice his mouth like an apple—
the mouth grinning
as it breaches the picture frame.

But he's already gone—leaving nothing
but a trail of scat for me to follow.

*[June 19, 1942—Portrait of Norma Jeane on her Wedding Day to Jim Dougherty]*

Instructions from my Aunt Grace
at the end of my high school sophomore year:

"Marriage or the orphanage, your choice
Norma Jeane."

If I say yes, the dress is iced in lace
& I am a ribbon-tied gift—a statue

in honor of {him}. In my brand-new
shoes, I am a hand me down. Pass

the green beans & I will mind
my peas & queue up for groceries.

I will whip up a wife for breakfast
& bake rockets & bathe

in his glory. & when night growls,
I will dutifully give him my promise.

*[1944—Yank Magazine Pin-Up of Norma Jeane by David Conover]*

There are so many men
& I find myself wanting

to shed even this flimsy skin
like a snake, reveal what lies beneath—

Instead, I trade
a shimmer of my skin for their letters—

the envelopes emptying as I swallow
each word from *dear* to *love*. Does the flash

tattoo my flesh with diamonds? Will I dazzle
& distract? Does the camera see *me*? See

the blueprint of my bones?
If I thrust out my hip,

will it save a life? & if I tilt my chin,
bite my lips? What then?

*[1952—Publicity Photo with Joe DiMaggio]*

How quiet he is in this swirling
room of cocktails. I flirt,

draw my lips into a perfect bow.
Amongst the swarm of lit tables,
do the two of us glow?

He sips Bordeaux, while I buzz.
How quiet he is.

I lean in—a flash of *White
Shoulders*, a show.
Joe takes my hand in his.

How small I've become—a firefly,
a moment, a cameo.

*[1955—with Ella FitzGerald at the Mocambo Club in Hollywood]*

My table close
enough to see her
diaphragm   accordion
each breath    licking
our ears   purring
down our throats
        curling

she sways    commands
        the spot light

her low notes throb
and we forget
our gin and tonic
cigarette    smoldering
        lust

*[Los Angeles, June 1956—by Cecil Beaton]*

His distant eye
sees into my future—
a surgeon unbuttoning
my skin.

A bed of cheap
carnations
& my promise
soon swelling
in water, rising
with acid. My startled eyes
fixed for all time as if to say,
*Please leave something*
                    *ablur.*

*[Los Angeles, June 1962—The Last Sitting with Marilyn by Bert Stern]*

Me in black.
If I am ever a widow,
I will mourn color.
I will weep for yellow narcissus
& grassy meadows ticked with cornflowers.
Let me stain my fingertips with cherries.

# Ars Poetica

I've been told I write too pretty—
my lines & images so beautiful,
my metaphors to die for.
*Write uglier*. I'm told. I say read
to the end.

I say, when I look in the mirror
I see a pretty girl. Reflect
on that a minute—on a girl
who's been told she is pretty
enough to be a star, a Jean Harlow.

I say look in the mirror, don't
you want to see beauty?
I paint mine on. Play
the pretty girl who rewrites herself

so frequently, I can hardly
keep up.

She says her lines beautifully.
She says my lines beautifully.
But it won't matter.
It still gets ugly.

1:22 am

Roll Camera Action

Hello.

It's me, Sugar!

It's me, don't you remember?

The tomato from upstairs.

## Good Morning

Maybe it's my birthday
or just the blinds blinking
into little sparklers. I have wishes
lined up like the champagne bottles
& cigarettes on the windowsill.

Last night, I rode a crazy pill to the moon—

& this morning, look in the mirror—
I'm flush, a mimosa tree all summer.

Well then, I think I'll eat toast
with apricot jam, powder my nose
with sugar, grind coffee into my brows,
brush nectarine on my cheeks.

Call it good, call it a day.

## Following the Script

The pills were the make-up
man & the hair stylist & the costume girl.
The pills were the trailer, the mirror lit with little lights
& the fridge filled with champagne. They made everything right—
no forgotten lines, no forgotten nights—or so it seemed
but I'd forgotten to get out of bed. Then I played it
straight for a bit.

Was it a week? A month?
Nights & days were never so bright. That LA light—
I saw palm trees again, fat-headed against the blue sky.
& Wilshire Boulevard was so glaring with shiny cars,
I had to close my eyes.

I had to close my eyes, but I couldn't without
the pills who whimpered in my medicine cabinet.
They followed me into the bedroom, leapt
onto the bedside table. They knew how to turn on
& off the lamp. How to work a room.

The pills were clever that way. They could glad-hand
into any handbag, could have had their own show.
They were producers all right.
Despite what everyone says, I follow
the script. I take direction.

## Selfie on a Bad Day

Today, I'm stuffed with doubt.
When I wallow, the neighbors look
away & it's too early for a cocktail or
even an aperitif, the sun high.
The kid across the street smoking
weed so I join my dog on the porch—
sniff the air & hope for a gust of ganja
or the weather to turn. For each bluebird day,
there's one gone to hell. A Libra balancing act.
For all the weight I've carried, LORD tip
the scales this way & if not, I'll need concealer—
the good kind & yeah, a dirty martini
& please O Exalted One, let me sleep
on anything but Ambien. But enough about me—
what's up with that big heart of yours?
Have you an open chamber that I could
crawl into & stay awhile?

I worry the edges of night.
Tear the stitches along the seam &
there's my ass. I've woken up in someone else's
bad dream. Possibly mine.

*~Sylvia Plath wrote in her 1959 diary: "Marilyn Monroe appeared to me last night in a dream.....She gave me a manicure...She invited me to visit during the Christmas holidays, promising a new, flowering life."*

Give me your bitten hand.
I will paint each moon sliver—
          Amaryllis red.

If you are a girl
swirled in the thick of a dream,

I am a play
of red-tongued wolves and barn owl howls.

Let me curl into your hair, crawl beneath
your winter. Scrawl me in lines.

Let me mean *everything* to you.

I promise lavender and honey cakes
and the taste of Christmas roses.

# Insomniacs' Slumber Party
*~with lines from a 1967 Judy Garland interview about Marilyn*

Judy:  It's so easy to forget.

Marilyn: Maybe I want to.
       Forget

Judy:  how many sleeping pills

Poet:  I've taken.

Judy: And you wake up in 20 minutes
       and forget you've

Marilyn: been asleep. So awake

Poet: in the middle of the night.
       I'm awake,

Judy: so you take a couple more

Marilyn: sleeping pills to sleep.

Poet: That's what they're for—to sleep,
       so

Judy: the next thing you know
       you've taken too many.

Marilyn: I've taken so many

Poet: to sleep. I've taken so many—

Judy: You shouldn't be left alone.

Poet: Leave me alone,

I just want to sleep

Marilyn: alone.

Judy: With too much—

Poet: we'll finally sleep.

Marilyn: Turn off the light, bunny.
                 Please let me sleep.

## Four Days at Payne Whitney Psychiatric Clinic, 1961
*~ with lines from Marilyn's letter to her psychiatrist Dr. Greenson*
*after being committed by Dr. Kris*

I scrape my body
off the scrawled walls.
Pinwheel on a stone
bed   carve my lines
into the steel desk

very very sick girl
hold that thought

phone gone
I call no one
call Joe
for old times sake
very very dark place
hold that thought

each act an act
a line spoken
a rule broken
a small token
from last year's movie
sometimes I wonder
what the nighttime is for

cut a girl said
she said she cut
I called cut
the scene cut
into lines across
the window cut
me in lines   open
that window
men are climbing to the moon but they don't seem interested in the beating heart
hold that thought

## 1:53 am

cut to interior black & white a girdle so loose she said
apple you big banana head she said diamonds edit film
goose-pimply she said grip hero herring in a little glass jar
she said fuzzy end of the lollypop she said gaffe hello
it's me she said hey where's my lasso giddyap she said

## Sometimes I Just Want to Be Norma Jeane

I slice myself in half like a lemon,
leave Marilyn in the vestibule.

Tell me,
is she peering

out the paned window
as I tie on my scarf,

settle my sunglasses
and step out in the half-

sunlit street? As I reach
the East River, could I

slip the railing and be pulled
on a barge out to sea?

We always leave each other
like this.

One or the other.
I tell her I need to walk,

shake the bones
that scuff under my flesh.

I don't tell her I may follow
the trail of autumn leaves

that color the sidewalk,
disappear—

## Earthbound

O lemon—
I know nothing so sweet.

Rough-fleshed fallen fruit.
We are so earthbound.

Standing, knife in hand.
Peels curl the sink. Juice

stings each slit, slight,
my skin sunlit.

Combustible as tinder,
a warbler's nest,

this short flaming life—

Seasonal Disorder

Fallen pears, still that yellowish green—
chartreuse sounds too fancy
for fruit that no one bothered to pick
in its moment of ripeness,
fat bottoms swollen, sugared.
Weighted branches heaving.

It will rain soon,
the fruit browning,
falling before the leaves
that already mimic
sunflowers in decay.

Can I hit the pause button now—stop
before I mark another year
without my father?

His absence on my shoulders
like the cardigan I carry around
just in case.

My mother's handbag bulges
a sweater, sewing and first aid kits,
bag of almonds, wool hat, umbrella.
You never know.

## Curating Death

When my father died, I wrote
his obit, said he loved his family

more than anything. After all,
he'd become us in the end. I think

of his face, the one I wear when alone—
if I'm ever alone in the tic tic

like Marilyn, alone—tic tic tic.

She asked for Judy Garland's
*Over the Rainbow* & champagne

silk lining her coffin. I want
ashes. Just ashes.

## 2:37 am

I hum like the dart & hover of bees in my lavender—
I hum like a car engine hums in idle
my heart hums, vibrating.
I count minutes, hours, each
breath, countries I've visited, men I've known.

# Hello, it's Me, Marilyn
*~August 4, 1962*


**4:16 pm**

Dr. Greenson are you there?  My ears—

                    I can't hear.

Dr. Engelberg left me a satchel of pills.
I've lined them up
          along the windowsill—
                         like a string of pearls glistening
                 round my neck.

I feel lost in someone's garden—
                    ivy and jasmine tangle
          a swarm of bees billowing
                 the lavender.
They honey & swirl the air.        I'm in such a mood.

Dr. Greenson,    come rescue me.

*7:10 pm*

Hello Peter, Dr. Greenson's just gone.

      A dinner party tonight?    Lovely
               but I'm tired, need rest.
Already in bed,

a mess.    It's late.

      I've nothing on.


I guess    if Bobby's going to be around, I could wear
      that Balenciaga gown,
have Whitey come fix my face.

It's been stung—
          my eyes, lips.

Bees everywhere.
      I know I sound crazy.
         They swarm.

Ah. No Bobby? I'll stay home.

Kiss Pat goodbye,
the President too & you
            sweet guy.

*7:27 pm*

Whitey, my prince.
No need to come over,
No President, no brother,
        no bother.

I'm staying in with my hive.
I'm their queen, pillowed
                    by the buzz—

Whitey my love, don't worry.
I'll sleep off this sadness.

        I promise
                    tomorrow.

### 10:23 pm

I dreamt I had a father
handsome as Clark Gable.

At night, he'd hum me
to sleep & I'd dream

I had a father
   who dreamt he had a daughter.

He found her
in the phone book
under pretty.

He found her
at the orphanage
in the city, lost
       amongst the wingless angels, piles
           of fallen stars.

He found her drinking
      (whatever's in style).

Daddy look me in the eye.

You know it's me,
your girl, the child
you've never seen.
Don't hang up, I'm your Norma Jeane.

### 10:49 pm

Hello little jellybean, hush baby child.

I lost you in the wilderness       when you fled
            like a rabbit.

I lost you in the ocean—
        when you swam
                with rainbow fins.

I lost you down the drain—
                a diamond ring.

I lost my grip
        on you sweet
                pink thing.

Shush don't cry.

I lost you in a pill box.

But shush
don't tell a soul.

        I lost you —
you were just a gust.

I lost you to the bees.
                My head's a buzzy hive.

They stung my babies
        & left me alive.

## *11:24 pm*

Momma,
remember me
         waving
from up in the fig tree?

You wore lemon yellow.
You laughed.

Remember that?

Before
   the bees.

Hear them sing—
      flickering
           wings.

## All I Ever Wanted

An ermine-lined raincoat & a pocketbook
of Barbiturates taken by the handful, washed down
with Champagne—fridge stocked with good bubbly.
I love Doctors too. A doctor a day makes the sad
go away. Everything. I want everything to be
swell for my Friends. My friends keep me alive,
they honestly do. God gave me a childhood from
hell & no father. But Heaven help me—
I have real talent & work I so love! I will never give it up.
Not for any Joe. Not even my Joe, my hero,
my savior. Nor for the Kennedy I've Kissed
(or two!). I suppose real love is rare. I fall in Love,
but there's not one man that I have truly loved. Men love
me, or they love Marilyn Monroe that is. Naked as a jay!
I don't mind naked—it's just skin. Open me up, you'll
find a woman inside who reads Poetry—loves it & jazz
& art & oh gosh, Arthur, he Questioned my intelligence!
Before I even met him, I'd Read his plays & all the great
books & at UCLA I Studied history. I'm a student of life.
Holy moly, if only Things had been different—Mama's brain
healthy & life's Ugly stuff like crap men & contracts, sexism,
addiction & Violence gone. But would there be a Marilyn
Monroe? Would she exist if Norma Jeane hadn't become
the X-rated beauty queen, sexual dream doll? & would
*You* be here reading my thoughts decades after a man
Zipped a bag over my thighs, breasts, baby blue eyes?

## 3:51 am

I name fruits: apple, banana, cantaloupe, date, elderberry.
I name car parts: axle, brake, carbonator, dashboard.
Cities: Amsterdam, Beijing, Copenhagen, Dakar.
Countries: Zambia, Yemen, x, Wales, Vietnam, Uganda,
I pee, take a quarter Ambien. Tanzania, Sweden, Russia.

# Late Night TV

In this episode, a celebrity comes to perform.
She's on mickeys, definitely
suicidal but has a perfectly sculpted body.
I'm not sure whether to pity, envy or be her.
I know *that* body is a non-starter. I'd need
breast implants, Botox & bleached hair.

In the rerun of this episode, I'm the host.
I've invited the celebrity to sit on the couch
to chat about all the serious stuff like sex
& drugs & her crap childhood
& girl you gotta spill on those men.

Thank god for a commercial break.
& when we return, someone's wheeled a bed
onstage & Martha Stewart is demonstrating
hospital corners. So Marilyn & I tuck
ourselves into the perfectly made bed
then kill the klieg lights.

take that bow then slag off


How is it I always find myself here face to face—
serum eye cream mascara brow liner blush & lipstick o lord

when did I become such a drag
queen of you
a cuticle away from a real tiara
& now I've forgotten my Dior dress
I left it hanging

c'mon let's toast to auld lang syne my friend
& the final cut in the can
hurry up please its time

be a good girl gulp your gin & grapefruit
while I drink a gimlet there is so much grief
in glamour

have you an opinion about genius
it's amazing what good cheek bones can do

now take that bow
then slag off
let the credits roll maybe there's a sunset

& I stride solo toward it   kitten heels in hand

# Then I Slept

First there was the lemon peel
of morning. Then the empty space

in the bed, still warm, my love's body
held in the slight indentation.

Then the clatter of his oatmeal and tea
and beyond that a neighbor's whistle,

a dog's rugged bark, a man
calling out as a car door slams.

I slept in, slept through the night.

I slept without Ambien's dark
fist pressing my pillow. Slept all night.

My love questions
God's existence, but I hear the weather

is warming this week. Our plum tree
is cotton balled, the heavy perfume

of daphne drifts through an open window
and a hummingbird whirs over the forsythia.

In the stacked white boxes
up the hill, the honeybees doze.

•

# Author's Note

In the summer of 2018, I set out to write poems in the persona of Marilyn Monroe claiming zero knowledge or affinity for the long dead actress. But I was keen to push myself poetically by writing in persona and intellectually, I wanted to explore our infatuation with celebrities and our performance culture. In Marilyn, I chose the most enduring, consistently iconic celebrity to inhabit.

In the course of writing *An Insomniac's Slumber Party with Marilyn Monroe*, I morphed from a place of distant familiarity with Norma Jeane Baker, aka Marilyn Monroe, to one of spiritual affiliation. By starting in the unknowing, I committed to arrive at an understanding of the fully fleshed human not by scraping beneath the known superficial celebrity, but by accumulating everything I could learn and then discovering my own 'Marilyn'.

At times I felt as if I were sculpting her from the detritus of her life and perhaps my own. I started by reading biographies and autobiographies of Marilyn, of Joe DiMaggio and Arthur Miller. I found the various accounts often conflicting. This led me to the Internet for specific searches of her history and the people in her life, the era she lived in and so much else.

I read academic papers on Marilyn, as well as scholarly writing on her influence on celebrity culture. On auction sites, I discovered love letters, photographer diaries and a vast world of the collected flotsam and jetsam of her life. I read fictionalized novels, plays and poems based on Marilyn and the reviews of these works. And I consumed essays written over the decades. I became a Marilyn geek. Then friends started sending me Marilyn stuff. Marilyn Merlot, anyone?

Online, I discovered troves of photographs taken over the course of Marilyn's life. In Paris, I visited the Galerie Joseph's *Divine Marilyn* exhibit of photographs. Eventually, I watched many of her films and captured hundreds of lines from her characters that I added to the dozens of quotes I had gathered from her or about her by others.

The resource I returned to over and over was *Fragments*, that is a compilation by Stanley Buchthal and Bernard Comment of Marilyn's journals, letters, poems and notes. And finally, I started Instagram and Facebook pages to understand her eternal allure with fans and to serve as a coda of sorts to my poetic investigation. This led to the enduring Facebook community and conversation @marilynmonroepoetryproject.

As I researched and wrote, Marilyn's voice became firmly rooted in my mind. I felt confident writing as Marilyn and I had *so* much material to draw inspiration from. In some of the poems, there are lines pulled directly from documents or films, in others just the remnant or ghost of learning remains. Beyond voice, I employed punctuation used by Marilyn and I constructed a language and image palette for her that is floral, fruity, colorful, dangerous— feminine, vibrant with a hint of violence.

While I set out to write as Marilyn, in the end the poems in *An Insomniac's Slumber Party with Marilyn Monroe* are a fusing of Marilyn and the poet as speaker, of two women's lived experiences and interior beings. The closer I came to knowing Norma Jeane Baker, the closer I came to myself. And isn't that celebrity's truth—as reflection and projection of oneself?

# Notes

"I see her everywhere—"
*Reticular Activating Factor* is actually misused in this poem and by the poet's mother. What is meant is the 'Baader-Meinhof phenomenon' or 'frequency illusion'. The Reticular Activating System is a set of connected nuclei in the brain that (ironically) regulates wakefulness and sleep/wake transitions.

"What I Give of Myself"
With lines from and inspired by Camille T. Dungy's poem "How She Didn't Say It."

"Refusing to Bow"
The quote from film critic Pauline Kael appeared in a *New York Times* book review of Norman Mailer's *A Biography* on July 22, 1973.

"Reading *Ulysses*"
With lines from James Joyce *Ulysses*.

"Selfie with Marilyn"
Inspired by the Diane Seuss poem "Self Portrait with Emily Dickenson."

"How to Throw a Communist Party"
An acrostic poem with lines taken from Marilyn Monroe's party planning menu, guest list and shopping notes (1955-56 journal from *Fragments*) appear in italics.

"There Was No Honeymoon"
"You ever think of getting married again?" is a line from *The Misfits*. "The sweet cantaloupes of (my) rump" is from a letter Arthur Miller sent to Monroe in 1956.

"What the Maid Witnessed"
Features lines from a maid's interview interspersed with lines from a poem Marilyn wrote while she was filming *The Prince and the Showgirl* in England (*Fragments*).

"After the Miscarriages"
With lines from and inspired by Marjorie Manwaring's "Letter from Zelda."

"*Divine Marilyn* in Paris"
The Galerie Joseph in Paris staged an exposition of 200 photographs and artifacts of Marilyn Monroe during the summer of 2019. The exhibition notes are based on some of the photographs on display.

"Ars Poetica" is for Catherine Barnett.

"1:22 am"
Marilyn Monroe film character lines from *Bus Stop* and *The Seven Year Itch*.

"Following the Script"
Inspired by Marie Howe's "Magdalene and the Interior Life."

"Dear Sylvia"
The full entry from Sylvia Plath's 1959 diary: "Marilyn Monroe appeared to me last night in a dream as a kind of fairy godmother. I spoke almost in tears of how much she and Arthur Miller meant to us (her husband and herself) although they could, of course, not know us at all. She gave me a manicure. I had not washed my hair, and asked her about hairdressers, saying no matter where I went, they always imposed a horrid cut on me. She invited me to visit her during the Christmas holidays, promising a new, flowering life."

"Insomniacs Slumber Party"
The lines attributed to Judy Garland are from an interview in *Ladies Home Journal* in 1967 where she discussed Marilyn Monroe. Garland also famously suffered from insomnia and accidently overdosed on June 22, 1969. The last two lines were delivered by Monroe characters in *Bus Stop* and *Don't Bother to Knock*.

"My Four Days at Payne Whitney Psychiatric Clinic, 1961"
Lines from Marilyn Monroe's letter to Dr. Greenson (her psychiatrist) written while she was committed to the Payne Whitney Psychiatric Clinic by her other psychoanalyst, Dr. Kris.

"1:53 am" includes words and lines spoken by Marilyn Monroe characters in *Some Like it Hot, The Asphalt Jungle, Gentlemen Prefer Blonds, The Seven Year Itch*, movie filming terms and a line from her acting notes (*Fragments*).

"All I Ever Wanted—"
An abecedarian that zig zags.

"Late Night TV"
With lines from and inspired by Jen Levitt's "Reality Show."

"take that bow then slag off"
Includes a line from T.S. Eliot's "The Wasteland."

"Then I Slept"
Inspired by Ada Limón's "The Last Thing."

On the cover photograph of Marilyn Monroe by Milton H. Greene: "Growing up in the entertainment business I was surrounded by artists of all kinds. A fundamental lesson I learned from my parents early on was to reward creativity. Marilyn Monroe always had a fondness for authors and songwriters and loved to write her own poetry. In that spirit, we support Heidi Seaborn and the pursuit of her creative spark." ~Joshua Greene, The Archives, Author, *The Essential Marilyn Monroe by Milton H. Greene*

# Acknowledgements

I'm grateful to the editors of the following publications where some of these poems, excerpts or versions these poems, first appeared or were honored:

*American Journal of Poetry*
*American Poetry Journal*
*Barren Magazine*
*Bracken Magazine*
*Beloit Poetry Journal*
*The Cortland Review*
*The Daily Drunk*
*Fjords*
*Frontier Poetry*
*The Greensboro Review*
*The Missouri Review,* The Jeffrey E. Smith Poetry Prize finalist
*Moria*
*The Offing*
*On the Seawall*
*PANK*
*Parentheses Journal*
*Plath Profiles*
*Poets Reading the News*
*Serotonin*
*Sheepshead Review*
*SWWIM*, prize finalist
*The Write Question,* NPR
Tucson Festival of Books Literary Awards
*Visible Poetry Project*, a film by Sarah Tremlett

And in *Bite Marks* (2021), winner of the Comstock Chapbook Award and the forthcoming anthology *I WANNA BE LOVED BY YOU, Poems on Marilyn Monroe* (edited by Susan H. Case and Margot Taft Stever, Milk and Cake Press, 2022).

*An Insomniac's Slumber Party* with Marilyn Monroe began when I commenced the NYU MFA low-residency program in the summer of 2018 under the brilliant leadership of Deborah Landau. I'm wildly grateful to the NYU faculty, my fellow students and especially my advisors: Robin Coste Lewis, Meghan O'Rourke and Matthew Rohrer for guiding the poetic journey that led to this collection. And eternal gratitude to my thesis advisor Catherine Barnett who helped me discover a few ugly truths buried in a mess of beauty.

Blowing big kisses to Kelli Russell Agodon, Deborah Bacharach, Desiree Brown, Anika Czander, Sophia Faskianos, Matty Layne Glasgow, Veronica Golos, Lisa Hiton, Peter LaBerge, AD Tenn and Lillo Way for staying up late to read *An Insomniac's Slumber Party with Marilyn Monroe* and for your wisdom, insight and encouragement. And to Catherine Barnett, John Freeman, Deborah Landau and Diane Seuss for your generous praise.

My writing life is sustained and blessed by the poetry communities of Folio Poets Society, the Hugo House, Poets on the Coast, Tupelo Press and Volta. Sending love and kisses to my editorial family at *The Adroit Journal*.

I'm indebted to [PANK] Books Poetry Prize Judge Elivira Basevich for finding *An Insomniac's Slumber Party with Marilyn Monroe* worthy of the honor. And massive thanks to Jessica Fischoff for her insightful editing, inspirational spark and vision for this book. To Chris Campanioni and the entire [PANK] staff, thank you for bringing *An Insomniac's Slumber Party with Marilyn Monroe* to life, and a shout out to Justin Hargett for publicity handstands.

Heaps of gratitude to my family: my mother, my siblings, my children and their loves, and Scott. Your love and good humor ensured that producing a book during a pandemic was a joyous experience.

And to Marilyn for light.